Your **E**nvironment

GLOBAL WARMING

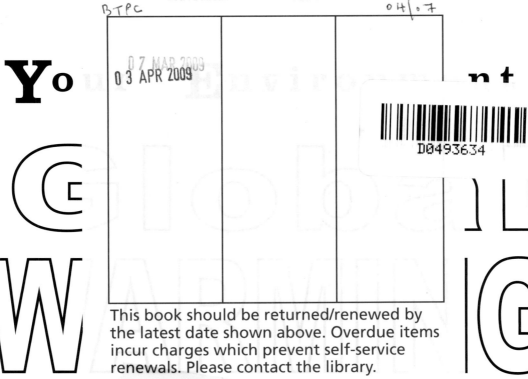

Franklin Watts
London • Sydney

How to use this book

This series has been developed for group use in the classroom, as well as for students reading on their own. Its differentiated text allows students of mixed reading abilities to enjoy reading and talking about the same topic.

① The main text and ② picture captions give essential information in short, simple sentences. They are set in the © Sassoon font as recommended by the National Literacy Strategy document *Writing in the Early Years*. This font style helps students bridge the gap between their reading and writing skills.

③ Below each picture caption is a subtext that explains the pictures in greater detail, using more complicated sentence structures and vocabulary.

④ Text backgrounds are cream or a soft yellow to reduce the text/background contrast to support students with visual processing difficulties or other special needs.

Introduction

Greenhouse gases in the ① atmosphere control the Earth's temperature. These gases trap the Sun's heat.

⬆ Global warming will ② cause some places to get hotter and drier.

This will affect the plants and ③ wildlife living in these places. ④

PAPERBACK EDITION PRINTED 2007
© Aladdin Books Ltd 2005

Designed and produced by
Aladdin Books Ltd
2/3 Fitzroy Mews
London W1T 6DF

First published in 2005
in Great Britain by
Franklin Watts
338 Euston Road
London NW1 3BH

Franklin Watts Australia
Hachette Children's Books
Level 17/207 Kent Street
Sydney NSW 2000

A catalogue record for this book is available from the British Library.

Dewey Classification: 363.738' 74

ISBN 978-0-7496-7531-8

Printed in Malaysia

All rights reserved

Educational Consultant:
Jackie Holderness

Global Warming Consultant:
Chris Osbourne

Design: Ken Vail Graphic Design

Picture Research: Gemma Cooper

CONTENTS

Introduction

The Earth is surrounded by a layer of gases known as the atmosphere. Some of these are called greenhouse gases because they trap the Sun's heat, the way the glass in a greenhouse does.

This process controls the Earth's temperatures. If the amount of these gases increases, the Earth can become warmer. This is called global warming.

◁ **Our weather will become more extreme.**

As the climate changes, extreme weather events such as hurricanes, heavy rainfall and heat waves can become more severe and unpredictable.

⬆ Global warming can change the weather and climate of the world.

Weather describes if it is raining, sunny or snowing, today for example. Climate describes the average weather conditions over a long period of time.

⬎ Our world is at risk.

The Earth has three main weather zones: tropical, temperate and arctic. Tropical zones are hot, with heavy rainfall certain times of the year. Arctic lands are very cold. Temperate zones are neither too hot nor too cold. As global warming alters climates, these three zones and their habitats become more at risk.

⬇ Global warming will cause some places to get hotter and drier.

This will affect the plants and wildlife living there. If it is too hot, plants may die, and animals will need to move to where plants can survive.

The greenhouse effect

All life on Earth needs the Sun's heat to survive.

The ideal temperature for life on Earth is 16°C (60°F).

To keep this temperature, greenhouse gases insulate the Earth, holding the right amount of heat to warm the atmosphere. This is known as the greenhouse effect.

⬆ Greenhouse gases may occur naturally or be caused by humans.

Carbon dioxide, water vapour, methane, ozone, nitrous oxide and chlorofluorocarbons (CFCs) are greenhouse gases. Landfills and cars, as well as volcanoes, produce these greenhouse gases.

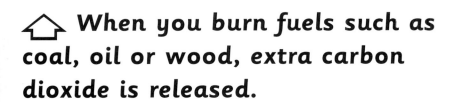

⬆ When you burn fuels such as coal, oil or wood, extra carbon dioxide is released.

These extra, man-made gases, like carbon dioxide, go into the atmosphere, trapping too much of the Sun's warmth around the planet. The Earth's temperatures rise. This is called 'global warming'.

◁ Rubbish and waste produce extra methane gas.

Methane is produced by wetlands, but also as rubbish and waste rot away. Leaving our rubbish in landfill sites increases the level of methane in the atmosphere.

⬆ Deforestation is helping global warming.

Large areas of forests and rainforests are being destroyed to clear the land and provide wood for fuel. Trees help our planet by absorbing carbon dioxide. Cutting down and burning so many trees means the level of carbon dioxide in our atmosphere is increasing.

A natural process?

Some scientists believe natural events can cause global warming.

They say that the Earth's climate changes naturally over time.

However, many scientists believe that these natural events are being affected by man-made pollution.

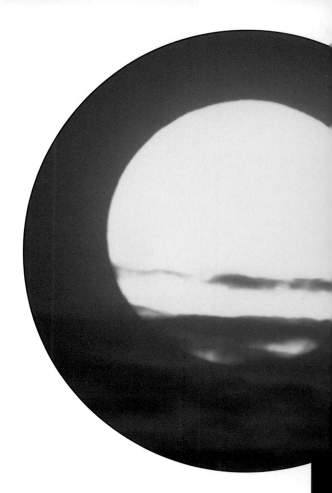

◁ **The Earth's climate changes naturally.**

About five thousand years ago, the Sahara Desert was grassland. During an ice age in the north, the Sahara had a temperate climate with plenty of rainfall. Prehistoric people hunted the land and hippopotamuses swam in the rivers. When the ice age ended, the climate warmed up quickly. The Sahara Desert was created.

The Sun affects the Earth's temperature.

The Sun's heat is never constant. Sometimes the Sun's rays are super hot, and sometimes they are slightly cooler. When these super hot rays pass through our atmosphere, their heat naturally increases the Earth's temperature.

This volcano is ejecting greenhouse gases.

Greenhouse gases are naturally produced. An erupting volcano produces water vapour and carbon dioxide. A large eruption would send more into the atmosphere.

Scientists know our pollution is increasing global warming.

For two hundred years, we have been cutting down huge numbers of trees and burning more fossil fuels. As a result, the Earth is warming up and summers are now becoming hotter. Floods and storms happen more frequently. The polar ice caps are melting. Within the last twenty years these changes have increased, so scientists know the Earth is warming up much faster than it would naturally.

The ozone layer

The ozone layer is a layer of gas around the Earth.

It helps to filter out the harmful parts of the Sun's rays.

Some years ago, scientists noticed that parts of the ozone layer had been damaged. In some places, there were even holes in it.

Scientists believe man-made gases caused this damage.

⬆ CFCs have been found in old aerosols and refrigerator cooling systems.

▷ A large hole in the ozone layer appeared over Antarctica.

Scientists believe harmful gases, called CFCs, created the hole in the ozone layer.

CFCs stands for chlorofluorocarbons. They used to be present in many products until it was discovered that CFCs were harmful to the ozone layer.

⬆ The ozone layer prevents harmful ultra-violet sunlight from damaging the life on Earth.

Life on Earth has evolved to live in the Earth's atmosphere. A change in the ozone layer that lets more light through could affect all life on Earth.

⬇ Does the ozone layer affect global warming?

Yes. Ozone is one of the greenhouse gases that are important in controlling the amount of heat in the atmosphere. CFCs produced by human activities damage ozone and have caused holes in the ozone layer.

If we can control the chemicals and gases we use, then we can reduce the effect these gases have on our atmosphere.

Fossil fuels

Fossil fuels are our main source of energy.

A lot of power stations burn fossil fuels to produce the electricity we need to live our daily life.

Every day we rely on energy to power our cars, trains and buses. So where do fossil fuels come from?

⬆ **Electricity is carried by cables.**

Much electricity is made by burning fuel to release energy. Developed countries rely heavily on electricity to run their factories, homes and schools. Now, developing countries are also increasing their demand for electricity and fuel.

▷ **Coal is one of the Earth's fossil fuels.**

It is mined from layers in the Earth's surface. Coal was formed by the compression of dead plants and organisms many millions of years ago. It is the most burnt fossil fuel.

This oil-rig is drilling for oil out at sea.

Oil is needed to make the fuel on which cars and lorries run. It is also used to make plastic and to heat our homes.

Oil is found under the land and beneath the seabed. It was made from ancient plants and creatures. Covered by mud, the pressure of layers of mud over millions of years turned them into oil.

Gas pipelines carry supplies of gas to be used in homes and industry.

We drill for gas and pipe it to our homes for use in heating and cooking. Like oil, gas was created from ancient plants and creatures and so is often found together with oil.

Atmospheric pollution

In the past, people used horses and carts for transport.

It was clean transport with no pollution.

After the Industrial Revolution of the 19th century, more factories, homes and cars appeared, producing pollution and extra greenhouse gases every day.

◁ **Cars and other transport add to global warming.**

Cars burn petrol, which releases extra carbon gas into the atmosphere. As the human population increases, more cars and other vehicles are on the roads.

⬅ The world's population increases all the time.

As the population grows, so does the demand for power. As we burn more fossil fuels we release more pollution into the atmosphere. It is important to find ways to provide power without polluting the Earth.

⬇ It takes a lot of energy to heat and light these buildings.

Cities all over the world use vast quantities of energy, provided by burning fuel. Electricity is needed to power computers, lights and heating. Look at the picture. Imagine how much electricity is being used to power the lights and computers.

⬆ This factory is polluting the atmosphere.

There are tight controls on factories and on how much pollution they can release into the air. Governments can fine companies if they release too many harmful gases into the atmosphere.

A polar problem

As extra greenhouse gases surround our Earth, the atmosphere and the oceans are warming up.

Ice is melting in the Arctic and the Antarctic. This means a loss of habitats for polar animals, and more water in the oceans.

▽Polar ice caps are shrinking fast.

The cold waters around Antarctica and the Arctic have become warmer in the last twenty years. Warmer oceans and warmer summers melt the polar ice, which will cause sea levels to rise.

◁ Penguin habitats are melting.

Penguins need large areas of sea ice to rest on and to raise their young, safe from the creatures that hunt them. If more ice now melts due to the warmer water, there will be less sea ice for penguins to live on.

▽ Rising sea levels will cause flooding.

When water is heated it expands, causing sea and ocean levels to rise. With extra water from melted ice, low-lying islands and coastal cities will be at risk from flooding.

△ Polar bears need cold weather to live.

During the Arctic summer, they travel long distances over the ice to hunt for food. They need to build up reserves of body fat to survive the cold winter. If more ice melts in warmer summers, then the Polar bears' hunting grounds will shrink. They may not be able to find enough food before the winter.

Beside and under the sea

Warmer water also damages life in and around the seas and oceans.

Under the sea, corals are at risk as the oceans warm up.

As the Earth's weather patterns change, more frequent storms will damage our coastlines and reefs.

▷ **Global warming is damaging coral reefs.**

Fragile coral turns white if the sea temperature around it is too high. This is called 'bleaching'. The coral will then die, resulting in a loss of habitat for marine life.

▷ **Coral reefs are important to both marine life and humans.**

Coral reefs are valuable ecosystems. They provide habitats for fish to live and breed in, as well as protecting coastal areas from storm waves.

⬆ Rising sea levels will flood beaches.

Sea turtles return to the same beach every year to lay their eggs. If the beaches are lost, turtles won't be able to find suitable places to lay their eggs.

⬇ Coasts and coral reefs are at risk from severe storms.

Tropical storms and hurricanes will become more frequent. These storms will damage coasts and coral reefs. The reefs will be broken up by storm waves, and coastal cities could be flooded.

Up and down the mountain

The higher up a mountain you go, the colder the air will become.

There is snow and ice all year round, even in summer.

As the temperature of the atmosphere rises, this cold climate will warm up.

▽ Mountain glaciers and ice caps are important sources of fresh water.

Glaciers are ancient frozen rivers of ice. During summer they melt a little, providing fresh water for the people, plants and animals in the foothills when there is little rain. When it snows in the winter, the ice freezes again.

⬈ Monarch butterflies migrate from America to the forests of Mexico for winter.

The cool, dry mountainous forests are perfect for Monarch butterflies. But if the dry climate changes, and there is increased rainfall, their habitat will become unsuitable and they may die out.

⬅ Plant ecosystems are changing.

As the atmosphere warms up cold mountain climates, plant habitats are changing. Alpine plants that are used to growing in cold weather are seeding themselves further up the mountain to escape the warmer temperatures.

⬇ Glaciers are melting faster in warmer summers and winters.

This extra, melted, water floods the lower lands, damaging villages and fields. Once a glacier has melted away, there will be no water for people in the foothills to drink and to grow crops with.

Extreme weather

We sometimes have thunderstorms, snow showers or very hot days.

But as global warming changes our climate, what kind of weather can we expect?

Already, some parts of the world are experiencing extreme weather for longer spells.

▷ **Water vapour is the most important gas in creating the weather.**

Warmer temperatures will cause higher water levels and increased evaporation of seawater. These water droplets will enter our atmosphere, raising the level of water vapour.

Hurricanes or tropical storms will happen more often.

Hurricanes need warm air and lots of water moisture in the atmosphere to form. With increased water vapour in our atmosphere, these hot tropical storms will become stronger and happen much more often.

Heavy rainfall will cause rivers to flood.

In 1999, Venezuela, in South America, experienced its heaviest rainfall for 100 years. There were landslides and floods that damaged many towns and villages. Thousands of people died.

Countries like India are experiencing extreme heat waves.

In May 2002, a heat wave struck in Southern India. The highest temperature was recorded at 48.9°C (120°F) and many people died because it was too hot.

Too little water

What will happen if there is not enough water?

Rivers and lakes will dry up and crops will be hard to grow. People and animals will be thirsty.

The land will become hotter and drier.

◁ **To produce corn as healthy as this takes lots of water.**

Crops need to be watered regularly if farmers are to make them grow. If there is not enough water, the crops will fail and people will go hungry.

◁ Hot and dry countries will experience more drought.

Many developing countries have hot and dry climates. Rain falls for a few months every year to fill waterholes and irrigate the land. If the climate becomes hotter and drier, rainfall will be scarce and water holes will dry up.

▽ This mosquito is finding newer, warmer places to live.

Mosquitoes carry diseases like malaria. Mosquitoes can live in certain hot places. As temperatures rise, mosquitoes are able to fly to places that used to be too cold for them. Now, people who aren't used to the diseases they carry will become sick.

△ It is important for us to not waste water.

You can help to save water by not wasting it. Even turning off the tap while you brush your teeth will save some of this precious liquid.

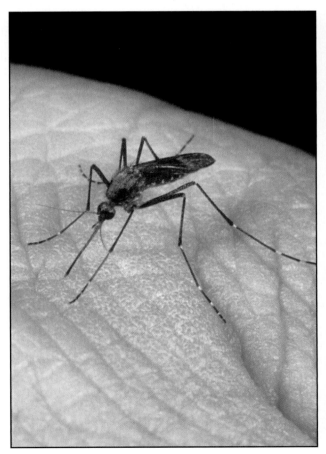

Too much water

Too much water in our seas and on our land can cause many problems.

Heavy rain or snow, flooding seas and warmer water are damaging to countries, habitats and even our sources of fresh water.

Too much of the wrong water can destroy an environment.

⬆ **Land habitats are changing.**

In Siberia, deeper snow has prevented grazing animals such as deer and boar finding grass. As their numbers decline, so do the numbers of Siberian tigers which feed on them.

◁ Deep water is not good for wading birds.

Wetlands are large areas of shallow water that provide a rich habitat for wildlife. Birds and other animals that feed here will be at risk if the water becomes too deep. They will be unable to dig for the roots and small marine creatures that make up their diet. If close to the sea, rising levels could poison the wetlands with salt water.

◁ Many low-lying islands are disappearing.

With higher sea levels and stronger tropical storms, islands like Fiji in the Pacific are being swamped by storm waves. Coastlines are moving further inland as the sea level rises.

△ Fresh water is being spoiled by salty seawater.

Humans, plants and animals all need fresh water. When it rains or snows, fresh water seeps through the ground into underwater pools and springs. When sea levels rise, salt water can also seep through the ground into our fresh water sources making them too salty to drink. This is called 'salt water incursion'.

Farming

As the world's population increases, countries need more land to grow food.

Forests are cut down and wetlands are drained to create crop fields. More farm vehicles that pollute the air are used to harvest more crops.

All this is having an effect on our atmosphere.

▷ **Farm vehicles produce extra greenhouse gases.**

When farmers plough the fields and harvest their crops, tractors and combine harvesters burn fuel and release carbon dioxide gas. Many farmers also use chemicals and pesticides that release nitrous oxide.

African farmers need lots of water to grow crops.

Parts of Africa are very hot and dry. Farmers have to irrigate their land to produce healthy crops to sell. Lake Chad in Africa is disappearing. Many scientists believe the lack of rainfall, combined with farmers using too much of the lake's water to irrigate crops, is causing the water level to fall.

Planting trees can help fight global warming.

To make sure that there are lots of trees to absorb extra carbon dioxide and create oxygen, many developed countries now plant a new tree each time an old tree is cut down. If new hardwood trees were also planted, over time the rainforests would re-grow.

Clearing forests for land is bad news for the Earth.

Around the world, rainforests and forests are being cleared for farmland and for fuel, to feed and power growing populations. This is destroying endangered habitats, and increasing carbon dioxide levels in our atmosphere.

29

What can we do?

In the last few years, governments have recognised the dangers of global warming.

They have realised that it is important to find other sources of energy instead of burning fossil fuels.

Many countries are trying to cut their carbon dioxide emissions over time, to reduce global warming.

But you can make a difference every day.

▷ **Turn off the light when you leave a room!**

Get into the habit of saving electricity. Switch off computers and televisions when you have finished with them to save power.

▷ **Finding cleaner energy like wind power will reduce global warming.**

Wind farms, solar panels and wave power are forms of 'green' energy that do not increase greenhouse gas levels. Recycling rubbish saves resources such as wood and coal from being burnt for power.

◁ Use your own energy whenever you can!

Walking and cycling, instead of using a car, is not just good for the planet – it is better for you, too! Using your own stored energy is important, so walk or cycle whenever possible, as long as it is safe to do so.

Look at these websites to find out more:
www.wateraid.org.uk
www.epa.gov/water/kids.html
www.panda.org/kids
www.climatehotmap.org

GLOSSARY

Climate – The average weather of a region.

Drought – Dry conditions caused by too little rainfall.

Environment – The natural world.

Greenhouse gases – Gases in the atmosphere that trap heat. An increase in the levels of these gases can cause global warming.

Irrigation – Watering the land.

Ozone layer – A blanket of gases around the Earth which filters out harmful rays from the Sun.

Pollution – Unwanted or harmful materials released into the environment, such as the gases released when fossil fuels are burned.

Population – The number of people living in a country or on the Earth.

Recycling – Reusing waste materials/rubbish.

Solar power – Using the Sun's heat to create power.

Weather zone – A group of places, all the same distance from the poles, with similar temperatures.

INDEX